James Morris Whiton

Reconsiderations and Reinforcements

James Morris Whiton

Reconsiderations and Reinforcements

ISBN/EAN: 9783741132322

Manufactured in Europe, USA, Canada, Australia, Japa

Cover: Foto ©Andreas Hilbeck / pixelio.de

Manufactured and distributed by brebook publishing software (www.brebook.com)

James Morris Whiton

Reconsiderations and Reinforcements

RECONSIDERATIONS AND REINFORCEMENTS.

By James Morris Whiton, Ph.D.,
Author of "Beyond the Shadow," &c., &c.

LONDON: JAMES CLARKE & CO.,
13 & 14, Fleet Street. 1897.

Contents.

	PAGE
"With All Thy Heart"	1
The Bed-Rock of Christianity	10
"Nature is Spirit"	20
The Mercy of God	32
The Intercession of Christ	42
The Generation of the Christ	53
The Lesson of the Leaf	62
A Talk on Immortality	84
Unspotted from the World	91
The Hidden Face	104
The Lord's Supper	113
Gymnastics and Ascetics	136
Jesus' Coming Again	143

Reconsiderations and Reinforcements.

"With All Thy Heart."

Martin Luther's wife asked him why it was that while under the Papacy they prayed more than after they broke from it. The answer is not on record. Emerson fondly recalled "those odoriferous Sabbaths" of the fathers as things bygone. Somehow the critical spirit has trenched on the devotional spirit, so that, as Professor Tyndall declared, to render due satisfaction to the religious sentiment is the "problem of problems" at the present hour.

Cool intellect, seeking the realism of mere fact, and warm feeling, seeking the realism of sympathetic life, move in divergent directions, and demand unlike satisfactions. Men in whom either of these two preponderates are wont to gibe at each other for one-sidedness. Whether it be possible for each disposition to obtain at once a full satisfaction is still in doubt. That they interfere to some extent is a matter of experience. Faraday, at once a scientist and a member of the Sandemanian sect, is said to have shut his oratory when he resorted to his laboratory, and *vice versâ*. But the mind is not built in tight compartments. The religious and the scientific spirit agree in the demand for unity. Intellect and feeling must coalesce in unity of thought. The characteristic of this is not mere reason, or mere feeling, but their conjunction in reasonable feeling.

But while this unity is not yet reached, and intellect and feeling are cultivated apart at each other's expense, there can be little doubt on which side a defect is more deplorable. Large intellect and little feeling is a combination less humane and truly human than large feeling and little intellect. The substance and staple of human nature is in its sentiency, its sensitive life. President G. Stanley Hall, one of the foremost of psychologists, remarks: "What constitutes life is the intensity, variety, and scope of what we feel." That it is feeling rather than intellect which constitutes man in the image of God, the Scripture suggests in declaring that "God is love." Love is intelligent, but intelligence alone is not love.

Morality, so far as it is more than the mere superficial behaviour which hardly deserves the name, is simply the cultivation of moral feeling—the active love of virtue, sympathy with good men, desire for a pure heart and life, together with heartfelt antipathy to all that stands in the way. Conscience is simply our comprehensive term for the mass of complex moral feelings which determine conduct. Religion is the same moral feeling, inspired by consciousness of its relation to the Universal Moral Nature which it recognises as the ground of its own individual existence. Thus the fundamental thing in human character is feeling, intelligent feeling, compared with which simple intellect is a fragmentary thing. Feeling without intellect makes a fool, but intellect without feeling makes a devil.

In the critical search of the intellect for the rationale of the universe and the grounds of knowledge, we must ever remind ourselves that these are not the things that our moral nature chiefly lives by. It is significant that both in Greece and Rome the period of the philosophers was the age of a decadent morality. St. Paul's terrible indictment of that moribund, because demoralised, civilisation is prophetic of what the world may always look for, whenever the needs of the moral life are turned over to the intellect alone or chiefly, apart from enlightened and sensitive moral feeling. "They became vain in their reasonings, and their *senseless heart* was darkened. Professing themselves to be wise, they became fools." Modern scientific researches have brought order into intellectual perceptions, but have contributed little to reform the moral disorders which are the scandal of modern civilisation. Modern experience is bitterly testifying to our militant industrialism and greedy mercantilism, that the understanding of all mysteries and all knowledge, apart from love, is, as St. Paul declared, "nothing" for the effective realisation of things of lasting worth.

Why is it now that, as Tennyson says,

> Truth in closest words shall fail,
>   When Truth embodied in a tale
> Shall enter in at lowly doors?

It is that in the "tale" Truth comes to the mind, not in the bloodless form of mere intelligible words, but with the warm touch of life upon sensitive nerves of feeling, awakening the response of active sympathy. Sympathy is the Divine anointing, without which the eye of understanding remains bleared or blind.

> And so the Word had breath, and wrought
>   With human hands the creed of creeds
>   In loveliness of perfect deeds,
> More strong than all poetic thought.

Where lay the failure of Calvinism? It overvalued intellect and undervalued feeling. Strong in logic, it was scant in human sympathy. Its Christ represented legalism rather than love. Grandly intellectual as it was, starved hearts revolted from it as cold and inhuman. It is possible for theological liberalism, in supplanting it, to repeat its mistake by offering the world that hungers for sympathy a one-sided intellectualism, with an undevout frigidity of feeling, from which the multitudes that long for the loving Son of Man will turn in disappointment away.

The grand truths which possessed Jesus with Divine power were truths realised in the deeps of His human feeling. He knew, but still more he felt, His brotherhood with every man, even the outcast. Equally He knew, and still more He felt, the truth from which this grew, His sonship to the Father of every man, sonship which in His consciousness was so real and eternal, that men incapable of sharing His thought of it charged Him with blasphemy for feeling it as He did. It was this feeling that He lived by, this that made Him

"Most human and yet most Divine."

In the awaking of this feeling in us also is the birth from above, of which He spoke; in its growth is the unfolding of the spirit's eternal life. To Nicodemus, greeting Him as a teacher come from God, Jesus declared that the teaching of knowledge by a master is not the fundamental thing, but the birth of this life from above in the pupil, the life that, awakened, grows toward Divine fulness in consciousness of that eternal sonship to God, which realises itself in sympathetic brotherhood to man.

Our vital problem is to feed this life of Divine sympathy with God and man, while the critical intellect is being fed with new information from old monuments and manuscripts and from the secrets of the physical universe.

Riches, whether in lands or in learning, often tempt us to forget Jesus' caution, that a man's life consists not in what he possesses. It is rather in what possesses him; but nothing possesses us that does not dominate the feelings. For the health of moral life, as evinced in the warmth and vigour of moral feeling, the great desideratum in this age of intellectual curiosity is to be possessed by a controlling sympathy with the spirit of a Divine humanity, as manifested in the life and death of the Divine Son of Man in the Gospel story. For a man's worth is no more than his worth of feeling is, and this is just what the object that sways his feeling is worth; whether it be property, or power, or knowledge, or, better far, a share in the Divinely-inspired struggle of mankind for a larger and purer life, as children of God and brothers to His holy Christ.

The Bed-Rock of Christianity.

WE once heard a preacher of some note make this statement: "Christianity is belief in a Book, *plus* mind; it is acceptance of certain documents, *plus* intelligence." This notion of Christianity causes scepticism in view of the unsettled questions raised by criticism of the documents. Nor can this scepticism be cleared till the provoking cause of it is done away, and the claims of Christianity freed of all dependence on any external authority like that of a book, however venerable, or however strong the argument for it in the court of the critics.

There are many who would disavow the statement of that

preacher, who hold the same idea in a less extreme form. They tell us that, in order to faith in Christ, it is first necessary to accept certain statements which the New Testament makes about Him, or certain interpretations attached to those statements by theologians. In other words, the authority of Christ for us rests on the authority conceded to the Book and its interpreters as vouching for Him. But this, at least, conflicts with the saying which the Book attributes to Jesus, that He was a competent witness for Himself, and needed no other. Reduce to its lowest terms the external witness that is offered for Christ; yet, so long as any of it is reckoned necessary to faith in Him, the way is open to scepticism about Him. Nor will that way be shut, until complete independence of any other evidence for Christianity than *Christ Himself* is substituted for the current fashion of appealing to the authority of the Book and its interpreters.

Now, of course, we must depend on the Book for *knowledge* of what Jesus did and said. But this is quite different from depending for the *authority* we concede to Him on the Book and its interpreters, as witnesses who must be sifted by criticism. Even those who insist most strongly on the testimony of these as necessary to support the claims of Jesus upon faith do not, in fact, ground their own faith, so far as it is real faith, on that. On the contrary, what convinces them is the attestation which their own conscience intuitively bears to the imperative moral authority of Jesus, as He is reported by the record of what He said and did. Invincibly persuaded as they may be that the record was made by infallible witnesses, this, which very few of them have verified for themselves, is not the real ground on which they accept Jesus as the Revealer of Divine truth. That ground is the verification which conscience itself gives them in its intuitive discernment of the Divine excellence of Jesus. Let the case be stated in the boldest terms; let one concede what hardly any sceptic would assert, that the Gospel sketch of Jesus is wholly imaginary, and that no such life was ever lived; it would none the less present us with an ideal of a morally perfect human life. But a moral ideal, once formed, is certainly authoritative for man's moral nature. Simply because it has *constructed* such an ideal, it is morally bound to aspire to realise it.

But, of course, the case for Christianity is much stronger than this. This ideal life has been lived. The aspiration which an ideal, once constructed, commands, is seconded by the natural impulse of admiration towards imitation of what has thus been brought within the bounds of reality. Nevertheless, we do well to estimate the authority of Christianity, even when reduced to its lowest conceivable terms, as the authority of a moral ideal, which needs not to be historical in order to be imperative.

Considering, then, that there is no genuine religious interest which is not also and essentially an ethical interest, it must be insisted that no such interest can be imperilled, it can only be promoted, by freeing it of all dependence on external authority of any kind. Only so can the ethical become independent, as it ever must be, of the non-ethical. The imperativeness of such a saying as "Blessed are they that hunger and thirst after righteousness," is not in the lips that uttered it, or in the pens that recorded it, or in the verification of the record by criticism. It is in the idea itself, as soon as presented to the conscience. Wherein lay the imperativeness of that saying for Jesus Himself but in the idea of it, as it rose in His consciousness from His communion with the Father? Where else, then, can be placed its ultimate authority for us?

But perhaps we shall be accused of forgetting that there are other sayings of Jesus, which are not thus immediately attested by the intuitive deliverances of conscience. As to many such, we must point out to the objector several things that he is in danger of forgetting, viz. :—

(1) These sayings belong to theology as the science of religion, rather than to religion itself.

(2) The truths they convey appear in connection not only with Christianity, but also with other forms of religion.

(3) It is not as a teacher of theological knowledge as a body of truth that Christ's fundamental

claim to be Master *begins,* but as a teacher of ethical religion as a spirit and life.

(4) In whatever theological knowledge Christ becomes an authority to us, it is through the experience of faith gained in following Him as authority in those prior concerns of ethical religion, in which conscience is His immediate and conclusive witness.

(5) There is a natural order in acquiring religious knowledge, which it is necessary to follow as in any other province of knowledge. To this Jesus refers us in insisting on ethical obedience as the condition of theological insight: "If any man willeth to do His will, he shall know of the teaching, whether it be of God." Without regarding this natural order we can get on in our theology no better than in algebra without first learning some arithmetic.

Here, then, we return confidently to our main point. The fundamental and specific claim of Christianity is not on the analytic and systemising intellect, but on that complex of moral feelings to which we give the name of conscience. To conscience Christianity presents itself as essentially a kind of life, a Divine life, eternal, *i.e.*, rooted in the nature of things, and cohering with the permanent order of the universe— a life which was realised in Jesus, and by Him is set before us as our moral ideal, that we may aspire to it and realise it, as the children of God, in an ethical fellowship of spirit and endeavour with Him.

This vital fact is to-day obscured, as for many centuries past, by the claims to external authority put forward by churches and by creeds. These fatally invert the natural order of religious progress by thrusting theological propositions in front of simply ethical and religious principles. Thus have they weakened the authority of Christ by bringing in that of the doctors and the critics, to stand between the conscience and that ideal life of the Master, which neither asks nor needs any witnesses to invest it with other authority than its own. The faith in Christ which relies on these, or any external witness whatsoever— even of apostolic men, as necessary to its full assurance, is so far not essentially an ethical faith. So far, also, it cannot be essentially Christian.

If such a faith is weakened, as its possessors sometimes complain, by finding its external evidences weaker than it had supposed, this is not to be regretted. For only so can a purer faith be substituted for it, by bringing conscience face to face with Christ's ideal of a perfect human life, through aspiration toward which is the only real salvation found in moral accord with the Master. Given such an ideal, whether historical or only imaginary, an imperative authority is felt therein by every conscience which is susceptible to the moral obligation of endeavour toward the Best that is disclosed to its vision.

But here—we must say it with all plainness—is the fatal weakness of much of the current scepticism concerning Christianity. Indifference toward the moral ideal exhibited in Jesus, repugnance to the strenuous moral effort which that ideal enjoins on conscience, is the hidden root of many cavils and criticisms, which are valued mainly as supplying excuses for not following the Master's arduous upward path of moral aspiration, as obedient children of God. They ask for more enlightenment, but that is not the one thing lacking to them—it is simply more inclination.

"Nature is Spirit."

So said Principal Fairbairn in a lecture at the Mansfield Summer School of Theology. To old-fashioned Bible readers it may savour of paradox. What sharper opposition in Scripture than "*natural*" and "*spiritual*"? But "the words of the wise are as goads." What if nature be spirit after all? But how can it be?

Of course, one must beware of the stumbling-block in the word *is*, over which there has been so sad falling in construing Jesus' saying, "*This is My body.*" The identity that *is* asserts is not the swamping of all difference. It is not absolute but conditioned identity. Nature is spirit in manifestation; nature is the utterance or expression of spirit; it is, so to speak, the "*Word made flesh,*" or Thought objectified in Form. What else could the philosophic lecturer have meant?

A pregnant saying like "Nature is spirit" condenses a volume of philosophy, and outlines a theology which requires large discussion and patient reflection before it can be domiciled in minds to which it now is strange. It logically involves an interpretation on the lines of monism, both of the universe and of human life.

How Dr. Fairbairn would unfold and apply his apophthegm does not concern us to inquire. But it is not intruding into private grounds to point out some apparent implications of it.

Nature and the Supernatural are not the two mutually exclusive realms that have been fancied. For supernatural we must substitute spiritual. The laws of nature are the ways of the Spirit, who utters Himself through the forms of nature. What men call miracle is no interference with nature, but the exceptional births or workings of nature moulded by the unknown powers of spirit. What men call revelation is not a communication to the world from without, but a development within the world, an unfolding of consciousness rather than a transference of knowledge. Providence, so called, is the orderly control of the world not by an external sway, but by the resident powers of the Spirit within the world. Prayer is converse with the Spirit in Whom we live, as really as from Him we are.

But this may be deemed going too fast for those who crave clear definitions. What do we mean by spirit? "The infinite and eternal Energy from which all things proceed," "the Power, not ourselves, which makes for righteousness," "God the Father Almighty, Maker of heaven and earth"—these terms, in which

Herbert Spencer, and Matthew Arnold, and the primitive Christian creed variously express the Reality which, in Paul's phrase, "is above all and through all and in us all," are definitions not too variant to stand indifferently for synonyms of spirit, albeit they are not all of equal value for our religious needs. What these terms variously adumbrate to thought is what we mean by spirit—the ultimate and eternal Reality that *is*, underlying all that transiently *appears*—the ground of the successively emerging and vanishing phenomena that we behold as nature, the things and beings that are born and die, the world that passeth away. This Nature is that Spirit—His perpetual utterance or word, His embodied thought.

Nature is spirit: this is as true of the cruder as of the completer forms of nature, and of what we call its wrathful as of its peaceful aspect. Matter, plant, beast, man, body, soul—"nature red in tooth and claw," nature in parental loves, nature in storm and earthquake, and nature in smiling harvest, is all of it spirit, if any of it is. The conflicting elements in human nature that we distinguish as spiritual, and as physical or animal, are distinct simply as higher or lower births of the one generating Spirit. All differences are variations, not contradictions, variations from the thin crescent to the full orb of the Reality that is back of all and in each.

Flower in the crannied wall,
I pluck you out of the crannies,
I hold you here, root and all, in my hand,
Little flower—but if I could understand
What you are, root and all and all in all,
I should know what God and man is.

From the primitive fire-cloud to the present world, from the jelly-fish to man, we see in nature the progressive utterance and embodiment of spirit from more to more. Nor can we draw any line, and say, there nature ends and spirit begins. Professor Rothe long ago observed, "If the Divine Logos can 'enter into' the *unconscious* soul, there is no reason why it should not 'enter into' an animal, a plant, a stone," &c. We trace the process of the Spirit through the successive stages of motion, growth, sensation, self-consciousness and God-consciousness, from the first movements of what we term matter—which physicists now say is in its ultimate analysis simply force — to those consummate unfoldings of the God-conscious life in which at length spirit is clearly recognised as both the goal and source of the whole.

Then it is seen that Spirit and Life are but two names for the one Reality which is in the whole and in every part. Dead matter, as we call it, is but comparatively dead, not lifeless; else there were no accounting for the unfolding of the fire-cloud into the living world. Its molecular pulsations are the throbs of the prolific Spirit, which gives birth to the successive forms of that nature which we distinguish in a comparative way into inanimate and animate. As Spirit, or Life, is one, so from first to last its process of utterance and embodiment is one. At length the event arrives in which the Spirit from whom the whole proceeds is most clearly declared. We call it "the Incarnation." Such it is in its preeminence of light and truth. But it is part of the process of which it is the crown—the process which without a break unfolds through what we speak of as the creation of things into what we recognise as the successive incarnations of life, in that hierarchy of animated existences whose visible head is man.

The truth that nature is spirit frees us from that dualism which has both confused thought and confounded morals by breaking the One Reality into separate halves—human and Divine, natural and supernatural, matter and mind, secular and sacred, God and a world external to Him, an infinite nature and a finite nature, and a Christ who is so inconceivably compounded of the two, that the Trinitarian has separated Him from humanity, and the Unitarian from Deity. In the recovered unity of thought we find the Infinite in the finite, mind in matter, the supernatural or spiritual in the natural, God in man, and a Christ who is one with us in the essential divinity of the human, yet diviner than we because more gloriously human. The uniqueness of the Christ is not hereby obscured, but rather the reverse, because translated from inconceivable to conceivable terms, according to that truly Biblical view of man which regards him as "the image of God," not as originally born such, but as ultimately perfected into such.

Two objections will be urged against this course of thought.

1. It is alleged to be Pantheistic. But not more so than the Christian Scriptures are. "*In Him we live and move and have our being.*" Not more is the unborn child in the mother. But it will be asked, What, then, becomes of our free will, our moral responsibility? We need not be concerned for this so long as our consciousness asserts, whenever we have willed evil, that we could have willed good. Not less certain is it that the finite spirit is dependent on the Infinite. The scope and limit of its freedom in this dependence are beyond us to determine. Enough to be conscious that it is above zero; that it is something. "Where the Spirit is, there is liberty"; the more of spirit, the more of liberty; hence

is man more free than brutes. But as Professor Seth observed at Mansfield, "Only from the standpoint of the Absolute can we be absolutely intelligible to ourselves."

2. The further objection, closely allied to the foregoing, alleges that this view of things ignores the sombre fact of sin. In thinking of God and sinners we meet a dualism that refuses to be reduced to unity. We respect, but need not fear, this objection. We have already allowed room for it in saying at the outset that the *is*, in "Nature is Spirit," does not affirm an identity in which all difference is swamped.

The question must be returned to the objector. What is sin? Certainly not a thing independent of God, for God has made it possible by constituting us what we are. The most patent fact in sin is the spiritual weakness which it evinces. Sin is the spirit's culpable weakness, exposed as such in experience, condemned as such in consciousness. Nature is spirit notwithstanding, though the spirit may come forth at first as frail as "an infant crying in the night." The dualism which then appears between God and the sinner is really in the antithesis of rawness to ripeness, "flesh" and "spirit," which is involved in the unity of the process of development. Not, of course, in the mere fact of this antithesis, but in the exorbitancy of it through the culpable surrender of the spiritual to the insurrection of the psychical or animal. Thus, as John wrote, "*sin is lawlessness*"—exorbitancy, a lawlessness which, as God made it possible, it is absurd to suppose He will not subdue in reconciling it to Himself.

The billows are many, but the sea is one. One Life lives in all lives. One Will works through all wills unto the revelation of the righteousness of God. "*The flesh lusteth against the Spirit, and the Spirit against the flesh, for these are contrary the one to the other.*" But none the less is each complementary to the other in fact, however contrary in quality and working, as an acid and an alkali. Each is the seat of a Divine energy; "nor soul helps flesh more than flesh helps soul." Each in its way works toward the unity which is ultimate, because it is also original.

Finally, the notion which, though slightly countenanced in the Scriptures, enters so largely into popular theology, of the corporate fall and ruin of all men in the person of the first man, is irreconcilable with the conviction that Nature is spirit, in that constitution of things which Science has discovered to be an everlasting process from less to more of life. In such a process redemption is essentially a constructive, not a reconstructive work. Redemption from what? From an imperfection which is aboriginal, not superinduced or intruded. Its process, therefore, is not the restoration of a lost unity, but the revelation of the unity that, though now latent and implicit, is both aboriginal, and ultimately to be revealed, when "*God shall sum up* [bring to a head] *all things in Christ*," and perfected humanity, "*full-grown unto the measure of the stature of the fulness of Christ*," shall be manifested as the Father's Eternal Son. Because Nature is Spirit, At-one-ment, or Reconciliation, is eternal, inwrought into the nature of things, for the merging of earth's discords in the triumphant revelation of God as "*All in all*."

It is noteworthy when so cautious and conservative a thinker as Principal Fairbairn announces a principle of so pregnant import for the modification of religious thought as "Nature is Spirit."

The Mercy of God.

"Also unto Thee, O Lord, belongeth mercy, for Thou renderest unto every man according to his work."—Ps. lxii. 12.

ONE is at first sight tempted to amend the Psalmist's saying, and for "mercy" to substitute justice. It seems characteristically just, rather than merciful, to render to men according to their works.

But let us emphasize the word *his*. Let us reflect that in what a man does there are elements which others have contributed, and for which others are responsible. It then begins to dawn upon us that some discrimination is possible, and that such discrimination is merciful.

When we separate from a man's work that which is not strictly *his*, but the work of his parents, or his teachers, or of the spirit of his times, even a bad man seems less culpable. Some, but less than all, of the wrong-doing that we see in him was really his. The savage who delights in torturing his prisoners, the persecutor who kindles the fagots for heretics, need the benefit of this discriminating word, "*his* work." Loss of sleep or dyspepsia may induce one to acts of peevishness or moroseness that are not wholly *his* work. The overworked pointsman who falls asleep causes a catastrophe not all *his* work.

These discriminations society cannot always make, and at the same time sufficiently safeguard public interests. But we may be assured that He who only is competent to unravel the complicated web does discriminate, and allots to each man retribution for no more than is strictly his. That there are such discriminations, however beyond our power to draw them truly, gives us a basis for charity, in our estimate of those who excite our intensest reprobation. When we see a Nero or a Borgia, and are taxed to account for such an excess of wickedness, we may reasonably think it represents the accumulated contributions of more lives than one, and a responsibility in which more than one has share.

Admitting all this, we must equally insist that no man can escape responsibility for the work which is strictly *his*.

We have to protest against a fatalism which some scientific men set up in place of the old theologic predestination. A man's work is determined, we are told, by heredity and environment. Given such ancestors, such an education, and such surroundings, the result inevitably follows. He is simply a product of his antecedents and circumstances, just like an apple on a tree. If we have to imprison him or hang him, it is not because he deserves punishment, but because we deserve protection.

People who tell us this do not always believe it. They, as much as any, are found exhorting men not to defy the forces of the universe, but to conform to them, and use them rightly. Evidently these exhortations are without reasonable ground, except as there is responsible freedom in those to whom they are addressed. This scientific "determinism," which regards nothing that a man does as strictly *his* work, is as one-sided in its view as the popular notion that all which he does is wholly his. One may say, if he will, that man is nine-tenths environment, but one must not cancel the residual fraction for which the responsibility is his. No ship is started on the voyage of life with rudder lashed. In the most ill-started, storm-crippled life, after all discrimination of the contributing forces which appear in the result, there is a certain remainder due to the free helm in the responsible hand—a work that is *his*, and a retribution due to that.

What we have now to observe further is, that not only is the Divine discrimination merciful, but the retribution is also merciful.

What should mercy seek first but to secure men against wreck and loss? And how can it secure them but by securing the moral order in its established lines of cause and consequence? We can do no more merciful thing for ourselves and our neighbours than to give the law of consequences full sweep, in rendering to each according to his work. Prudence, energy, honesty, fidelity, while they are in the stage of gristle, before they have set into stiff bone, all depend upon the operation of this law to brace them against temptation, as a sapling depends upon a stake to brace it against the wind, till it has become a tree with inflexible trunk. In the education of children it is of the highest moment that every violation of domestic law should be followed, not indeed by the brutalising rod, but by some proportionate deprivation of the benefits and comforts accruing to the obedient only.

To interfere, under however good a name, with the necessary brace of a growing character that is supplied by the law of consequences, is not mercy but murder. For a man to imagine that he can lie, or steal, or scamp his work to his neighbour's damage or danger, and escape the evil consequence, or any part of it, is to think the most immoral and dangerous thought. And it is merely helping somebody to think such thoughts—taking down the guard-rail on the path along the edge of the precipice—when we allow a weak sympathy to interfere with the hand that is laying on some guilty back the scourge of just consequence.

Is there, then, no place for leniency? May not one say with King Arthur in excusing Sir Bedivere—

> A man may fail in duty twice,
> And the third time prosper?

Unquestionably; and yet who will gainsay that, as things go, the danger is not of too little leniency, but too much? No doubt it sounds charitable to say, "Let him off; he won't do it again." But mercy demands security for that, not only for society, but for the wrong-doer himself. Nature takes this security of us by enforcing her rule, *Pay as you go*. Plato profoundly remarks: "That it is better for a man to be punished than to escape. It saves him from a worse punishment in the degradation of his character." So in Mrs. Ward's

"Marcella" Raeburn says of the homicide Hurd: "I believe that if the murderer saw things as they really are, he would himself claim his own death as his best chance, his only chance, in this mysterious universe of self-recovery." To maintain moral worth, to save manhood from degradation, true mercy prefers the sound way to the soft way, and renders to each according to his work.

What, then, becomes of the forgiveness of sins? Certainly, no cancelling of the spiritual law, *"whatsoever a man soweth, that shall he also reap."* Forgiveness works no cut-off of consequences. Like a pointsman on a railway, forgiveness shifts the train of consequences from a down grade to an up grade, from direction toward the outer darkness to the Father's house. It is the transformation of the consequences which issue from our indestructible past that forgiveness effects.

The moral law according to which forgiveness works is analogous to the scientific law of the persistence of energy with convertibility of force. The evil deeds which cannot be annihilated, and whose causative power must abide in our life either for evil or for good, cannot be cancelled by forgiveness, but only converted from a fatal to a vital issue. So the muck-heap, which above ground poisons the air, fertilises the soil when put under ground. The evil that is buried by forgiveness becomes a source of fruitfulness to the new-sown seeds of better resolution. This is that "covering" of sin which the Bible speaks of as effected by forgiveness. This it is for which we pray, if we pray intelligently, in the petition which Jesus taught us: "*Forgive us our debts.*"

The Intercession of Christ.

THIS is very plainly asserted in the New Testament, and is a matter of undoubted belief among all Christians. Yet it is equally certain that not all Christians have the same idea of it, or would explain it in the same way. It is not uncommon for them to ask each other, What do you understand by the intercession of Christ? Ministers are not infrequently requested to answer this question for the satisfaction of some honest doubter.

But how do such doubts arise? In former ages, when painters of the highest fame did not hesitate to portray the Almighty Maker as a majestic and venerable old man, it was easy to construe literally the apostolic teaching, that "*we*

THE INTERCESSION OF CHRIST. 43

have an Advocate with the Father, who ever liveth to make intercession for us." But the literal sense of such terms is to modern intelligence as inadmissible as that of the Old Testament phraseology, which speaks of God as "repenting" of a purpose to destroy the Ninevites. Many are more or less conscious of this, and still are no less certain that in some sense, to them mysterious, the perpetual intercession of Christ is a truth to be held precious.

The language is certainly figurative, for it calls up to our minds the familiar figure of the ordinary intercessor, who pleads for some petitioner, and gets some indulgence for him, which the grantor would not have conceded, but for the influence thus brought upon him to change his previous mind. Such a conception might apply to the Homeric and Vergilian ideas of Jupiter, alternately besought by Juno and Venus on behalf of

Greeks or of Trojans, but it has no place outside of heathen mythology. Jesus Himself warned His disciples against so thinking of God, telling them that the Father knew their needs, and could be depended on much more than earthly parents to hear His children's prayer. He went further. After He had said, "*I will pray the Father, and He shall give you another Comforter, even the Spirit of Truth,*" He added, as if to exclude the notion that His prayer would be the inducing motive with the Father, "*I say not, I will pray the Father for you, for the Father Himself loveth you.*"

All prayer for another is intercession. We pray, and so intercede daily with God for all whom we remember in our prayers. Jesus, in this respect, as in others, set us the example, when He declared that He should pray for the friends He left behind Him in the world. Nor can we think of Him as our solitary, though our chief, intercessor there: all those there who share His Spirit must be thought of as sharers in His prayer for us. These heavenly intercessors John saw in his vision of the "*golden bowls full of incense, which are the prayers of the saints.*" Our beloved, who prayed for us on earth, must be thought of as still praying for us above. The Christly Spirit is evermore an interceding spirit; Jesus's declaration originated the apostolic doctrine of the perpetual heavenly intercession. But evidently He did not, and we should not regard intercessory prayer, whether ours or His, as presenting to God any ground for gracious action in response other than that which God already has in the love He eternally bears us. Thus the very source of the doctrine of the intercession of Christ points us away from the misunderstandings out of which the graver doubts arise.

The same objection, however, arises against intercessory prayer for others, whether by us or by Christ, that is sometimes urged against any prayer for ourselves. If God loves us well enough to be gracious to us apart from our praying, what is the use of praying? Without raising the question whether such an objection does not often arise from an indifference of heart toward God, one answer among several may serve for the present.

God's will accomplishes itself through many intermediaries, such as the forces of nature, and the wills of men. He not without us, and we not without Him who works through all, bring aught of good to pass. If a blessing is to come to us, it is important that our will should work toward it with God. Prayer is a contributory force, because it links, or tries to link, our will with God's will in the humble committal of desire and endeavour to His control and direction. We spread our wants and desires before Him in prayer, not as if He knew them not, or cared not except for our importunity, but that we may view them as in His sight, and come to His mind about them, and work for them in His way and with Him if we can. This is the contributory part of prayer among the intermediaries through which God's will is accomplished. It seems to follow that the more prayer there is, the larger the result must be. The more co-operators, the more intercessors, the greater is the sum of concurrent forces, the consensus of wills working that way.

Among these wills, more or less intelligent, enlightened, persevering, and, in that measure, more or less efficient intermediaries of the Divine will, is the Divinely anointed Leader of the praying host, in human sympathy with each and all, our Master in prayer, as well as in faith and love and duty. He also prays with us and for us. His example is our inspiration, and a sure ground of confidence when we follow Him in this as in other things.

But this does not exhaust the subject. The special difficulty has yet to be met. We must say, as the foregoing line of thought requires, that God's will is not effected without prayer as it is with prayer, any more than it is effected without various other forms of co-operation with Him. But prayer, whether intercessory for others or for ourselves, suggests to some minds the idea of an activity external to God, and affecting His action by an influence not His own, precisely as the mythologists represent the heathen gods as wrought upon by the petitions of their votaries. We do well to reject such a notion. The

New Testament idea of prayer is, that it does not originate in man, but in God. It is through His promptings that we are moved to pray. Our aspirations are first His inspirations. Whatever force there is in prayer is generated not by us, but by the Spirit of God. Earth-born, it is heaven-begotten, not an activity external to "Him in whom we live," but, as the poet tells us—

> Prayer is the breath of God in man,
> Returning whence it came.

The same is as true of Christ's prayers as of ours. He repeatedly insisted, "*I can of Mine own self do nothing.*" He repeatedly declared, "*I speak not of Myself, but the Father that dwelleth in Me.*" In His prayers we must recognise the regurgitation of the Spirit of the Father into the Divine deeps out of which it issued to flood His soul. If we view His intercession as prayer, it is influential with God because originating in God.

There is still a view of the subject to be taken which is independent of the function of that prayer which God at once inspires and accepts. What God does He does for ever, because what He is He is for ever. In His unchangeable goodness "*He cannot deny Himself.*" Every act of God is a word which abides for ever. As the sweep of any circle is determined by however small an arc of its circumference, so any act or word of God in the past is a guarantee of our faith for all the Divine future. Thus reasons Paul: "*He that spared not His own Son, but delivered Him up for us all, how shall He not with Him also freely give us all things?*" The advent of such a Saviour as Christ upon the scene of human want and woe is a mighty act of God, a word that is an everlasting pledge. The hope founded on such a pledge might be dramatically expressed by the figure of an all-powerful intercessor, as in Paul's impassioned exclamation: *"Who is He that condemneth? It is Christ that died; yea, rather, who is risen again; who ever liveth to make intercession for us."*

There is no fault to be found with such a figure, but only with those who forget that it is a figure, and confound metaphor with reality. If we ask, then, in this view of the subject, what is the prevailing power which is figured as the intercession of Christ, we answer that it is God's inherent necessity to be true to Himself, because of which the grace that came once by Christ must be followed by grace for evermore, as often as we seek it, grace not only to the seekers, but, as before in Christ, grace even to those that sought it not. *"The Father is in Me,"* said Jesus, *"and I in Him."* Not only *"was God in Christ,"* as Paul said, but Christ was in God. Christ in God, then, when Jesus was on earth, is Christ in God now and for ever. This is the interceding power, the Christ that is in God, the love that *is* before the world was. Thus, as Paul triumphantly concludes, "*God is for us,*" Himself our eternal Intercessor, ever seeking to come between us and the things whereof our consciences make us afraid.

The Generation of the Christ.

"The book of the generation of Jesus Christ, the Son of David, the son of Abraham."—MATT. i. 1.

THESE words open the New Testament with a phrase borrowed from the Book of Genesis. The chapter which follows them is a condensed summary of the genealogy of the Christ which runs through the Old Testament history. What the Old Testament is in an amplified and illustrated form, this first chapter is in a succinct and specialised form, *"the book of the generation of Jesus Christ."* This phrase turns our thought back from the New Testament to the Old as to a sort of family history, a unique sort, a history of the development of spiritual life in a well-marked genealogical line.

There is an advantage in this view. It is as open to the unlearned reader as to the scholar. It is free from all the difficulties which beset critical study. When or by whom the component parts of the Old Testament were written from century to century, and when or by whom they were selected and put together as now, is of no consequence in this case. All agree, however, that the volume was compiled centuries before any one could have seen in it the generation of the Christ. When we have seen that such it is, we shall see how it came to be such —whether by a chance concourse of fragments, or by the Wisdom that made the worlds.

The Divine grace that is to work everywhere must begin somewhere. If the Christ is to be born for all nations, some one stock must be cultivated to bear

Him. The selection and the cultivation of this stock for the generation of the Christ are the theme which gives the Old Testament its singular unity.

First, as to the selection of the stock. Of the children of Adam, of Noah, of Terah, three sons are named in each family, and one is selected, who becomes the progenitor of the line blessed with Divine revelations. In each family and every case a prophetic voice inspires a presentiment of hope in a blessing to come in the selected line. In like manner Isaac is chosen, and then Jacob, and then Judah. More and more distinct and individualised becomes the prophetic voice, which in each case marks off the selected line from its collateral branches. To Abraham, the son of Terah, it is said, *"In thee shall all nations of the earth be blessed."* And when at length, out of the thousands of Judah, David is selected from among the sons of Jesse, the kingdom before promised to Judah is foreshadowed to him as a kingdom not to pass away : "*Thy seed shall inherit the kingdom for ever.*"

These oracles, heard at every fork of the growing stem, mark a consciousness of the Divine guidance of the unfolding development. Imbedded in different strata of ancient documents, compiled and edited by unknown hands, preserved in records or traditions of divers times and places, these oracles, and the successive selections they commemorate for the perpetuation of a stock of brilliant destiny, give a singular unity to the whole. Even more singular is it that they were gathered for transmission in their present form by Ezra's feeble colony among the ruins of Jerusalem, four centuries before the great Birth in which this unique hope found its surprising fulfilment.

Secondly, the culture of this

selected stock is no less remarkable. We note these stages:

(1) The formative stage, in which the family of Jacob grows into the nation of Israel in the sheltering bosom of Egypt, while its home in Palestine was inundated by Hittite conquerors. (2) The stage of instruction, begun at least under Moses, with an initiation into the fundamental principles of religion and morality in the Ten Commandments. (3) The stage of discipline through conflict, by which the independent tribes were welded into the Davidic kingdom, as a fence about the stock of promise.

But now, as if to show that the promise to David's line of a *"kingdom for ever"* referred not to kingdoms of the world that come to nought, there straightway sets in a political decline, singularly paralleled by a rising of spiritual power in the prophets, the unique glory of Israel. The stormier the political horizon, the clearer the prophets' vision of Israel's coming Law-giver, and His righteous, world-wide sway. The Assyrian conqueror absorbs five-sixths of the nation, but a church, a nucleus of spiritual men, is formed by Isaiah within the remnant at Jerusalem. This it was which, as an ark, outrode the deluge that engulfed the throne of David, and brought back again from exile the chosen stock in a well-sifted band, with its oracles of hope, now more luminous than ever in the glowing assurance of the second Isaiah.

Here the book of the generation of the Christ, as constituted by the Old Testament writings, is substantially complete. Selected, instructed, disciplined, the natural stock has become a spiritual stock. Weak in worldly power, strong in faith and hope, it is now waiting for its time to bloom. Nor was it unprolific, that pre-natal waiting time between the Testaments. Then the Israelite, dispersed among the Gentiles with his faith, his book, his house of prayer, his Messianic hope, prepared the way for the advent to all nations of the spiritual Law-giver of all.

"*But when the fulness of the time was come, God sent forth His Son.*" The spiritual stock, the product of all this selection and culture, the object of all this hope from immemorial times, is crowned at length with its consummate flower in "*Jesus Christ, the son of David, the son of Abraham,*" born not for His nation only, but for mankind. To signalise this fact the nation that had given Him birth expires as a nation almost in the very act, bequeathing Him as its great legacy to the world.

Criticism has modified our views of the Old Testament writings. It has shown them to be a gradually developed literature, which has experienced the vicissitudes of time, and is not free from the imperfection to which all literary works are subject. The more clearly this is demonstrated, the more impressive is the fact that such a literature, the product of centuries of growth and change, was brought into its present form, as the book of the generation of the Christ, four centuries before the birth of Christ, like a cathedral waiting for its spire. The Book and the Person attest each other as the fruit of one increasing purpose for the revelation of the grace and truth of God in the spirit and life of man.

A gracious feature of this book of the generation of Christ is the kindly notice it takes of those whom theologians have treated severely as the "non-elect." Seth is selected from among Adam's sons, Shem from Noah's, Abraham from Terah's, Isaac from Abraham's; Jacob is preferred to Esau, and Judah to his brethren.

Yet, before the history of the chosen line goes on, the non-elect are kindly remembered in various notices, as not disinherited, although passed by. Their homes and descendants are recorded. Esau also has his blessing, and all the sons of Jacob theirs. How different this from the proscriptive Protestant tradition, which regarded the non-elect as devoted to perish! The chosen stock was selected for an inclusive service rather than an exclusive privilege, "*that the blessing of Abraham might come on the Gentiles.*" The distinction between the elect and the non-elect is between benefactors and beneficiaries. When the blessing which the selected stock is cultivated to bear is fully ripe for distribution, it must be distributed. We may be confident that He with whom is no respect of persons has neither favourites nor outcasts, and ultimately equalises all men's shares.

The Lesson of the Leaf.

"We all do fade as a leaf."—Isaiah lxiv. 6.

As Christ drew a lesson from the lily, so may we from the leaf. Yet the words of the prophet, "*We all do fade as a leaf,*" may lead our thoughts in a different way from his. These words were originally spoken in lamentation over the wrecked glory of the temple and city of David, as devastated by Nebuchadnezzar with fire and sword. No fitter similitude of the sad change could the mourning prophet find than the faded leaf. Those dilapidated walls, those fire-scarred ruins of Jerusalem and Zion, brought to his mind the magnificent creations of the shepherd king and his illustrious son, only as the crushed and blackened leaf recalls the image of the glorious crown of spring. But to us the lessons of the fading leaf become spiritually instructive, as we bring to bear the light which science has afforded us respecting the nature and the uses of its short life, the meaning of its fading, and the real significance of its death. We learn that *the reality is different from the seeming*, both as regards the life of the leaf and its death. We find a nobler meaning in the life of the leaf, and that imparts a nobler meaning to its death. And the lesson thus derived brings us consolation and strengthening, as we apply it to some of the sadder experiences of mortal life.

The fading of the leaf seems to be only decay, only the blighting of a beautiful creation that existed only to be seen and admired. It seems nothing but the wreck of a thing that lived only to enjoy life, to bask in the sun, to dance in the breeze. And when the leaf's delicate tissue has grown hard and wrinkled, when its regular outline has been notched and broken, when the blast tears from the twig, and tosses aloft, as toys of the tempest, those cracked and shrivelled and discoloured things that once composed the forest's kingly crown, it seems only the dreary ruin of a life as gay and unsubstantial as it was beautiful. And this has made the fading leaf the poet's emblem both of fallen greatness and of the frail and fleeting nature of every earthly charm. And so the poet writes :

The melancholy days are come, the saddest of the year,
Of wailing winds and naked woods, and meadows brown and sere;
Heaped in the hollows of the grove the autumn leaves lie dead.

Thus the poet speaks of appearances, but botany tells us that, in reality, the leaf creation is not the objectless beauty it may appear to be, whose fading calls for pity and regret. It is for more indispensable uses than mere decoration and enjoyment that the leaf lives its short life, a life whose grand beneficence, as it rounds upon our view, redeems its end from pity or dishonour.

For the tree itself, says the botanist, the leaf " is both stomach and lungs." A single elm has been computed to possess in one summer five acres of leaves; each leaf a wonderful tissue of nerves and pores and cells and veins. In these countless cells, invisible to the unassisted eye, the sunlight enables the living plant to do its work. In these cells the mineral matter ascending from the roots dissolved in the sap, and the gaseous matter absorbed through the pores from the air, are mingled, and converted by the chemistry of the sunbeam into food for the tree. This then is carried by the leaf-veins into the twigs, adown the branches and the trunk, and is deposited under the bark in a ring of woody fibre. Another portion also goes to form the nutritious fruit, and another the reproductive seed. Thus the frail leaf, gay, beautiful, musical as it is, is yet ever at God's work, providing man with material for the necessities, comforts and luxuries of his life. The coral insect builds up in watery wastes those island homes which we find peopled by barbarous heathen. The leaf prepares the timber, canvas and cordage of the ship, which carries to these outcasts the Bible and the blessings of civilised Christian life. It prepares the substance of the sacred page on which the Divine message is imprinted; it prepares the food which sustains the life of the Christian herald on his errand of love. Most true, in Creation as well as in Redemption, is the Apostle's saying, that "*God hath chosen the weak things of the world, and things which are despised hath God chosen.*"

But this is not all of the useful duty to which God has chosen the fair and short-lived leaf.

The gas which the leaf-cell sucks from the air, and helps to change into fibre, is poisonous to animal life, and must not accumulate in the atmosphere. The same office that the coral insect performs for the sea, to keep the great fountain of waters pure, the leaf performs for that aerial ocean from whose pure tides we drink our life. "The oak," says Holmes, "is but a foliated atmospheric crystal deposited from the aerial ocean that holds the future vegetable world in solution." A mark of dignity has the Creator bestowed on all useful labour, however humble, by giving the glory of the forest, and the beauty of the many-coloured coralline gardens beneath the waves, to organisms that discharge for Him the duty of scavengers! The carbonic acid gas produced by all our fires, and by the myriads of breathing creatures, is absorbed from the air by the leaf through its countless pores. In the leaf-cells this noxious element is decomposed; part is worked up into food for the tree, and the residue, containing all that is fit for animals to breathe again, is given back to the vital air. Measure, if it were possible, by cubic feet of wood, all the trees upon the globe. Nearly one-half —forty-five per cent.—of the whole mass is the solidified poison of the atmosphere, extracted by the subtle chemistry of the leaf. How grandly beneficent is its humble life!

Nor is this all:

The leaf draws water from the ground through the thousands of tubes in its stem—eight hundred barrels, says a scientist, from every leaf-covered acre every twenty-four hours. This it gives out to the atmosphere in the form of invisible vapour, to be condensed into clouds and fall in showers—the very water which, were it not for the leaf, would either escape in freshets or filter through the ground to the caverns below. Thus the leaf works to bring upon the earth the early and the latter rain. It works to send the streams adown the mountains to the thirsty plains. It works to feed the rivers that turn the wheels of factories. And thus a thousand wants are supplied, commerce stimulated, wealth accumulated, comforts multiplied, and the leaf is made by God to be the silent, humble feeder of all this prosperity.

And now comes on its change. But now we see that this change is not the fading and the fall that it seemed, of a beauty outworn in idleness, and faded by flaunting in the sun, and claiming such pity as we give the butterfly surprised by frost. It is a change that comes most naturally and honourably, as the leaf fulfils its beneficent tasks. It is in and by its useful work, that the leaf changes from the pulpy thing it was in May to a thing of firmer texture. And so we learn to look upon it rather as a ripening than a decaying, when, as its work draws near the end, it begins to borrow less from earth and more from heaven; when it changes its work-day green for the holiday reds and yellows of the flaming sun; when it shares with the fruits it has humbly elaborated all the brown and ruddy and golden tints of the ripening time. The splendours of October, surpassing the tenderness of May and the sober dignity of August, fitly crown the close of a life that has been so useful. God grant our lives such heaven-sent ripening, through usefulness that lives to serve our Divine Redeemer's ends!

Let us now take up the truth taught us by the leaf into the higher regions of the experience of the soul. There, too, the reality may be other than the seeming. There, too, to rectify our view of life will be to rectify our view of death.

What is the life of the leaf? The child replies: To dance in the sun, to play with the breeze, to listen idly to the song of birds. What, then, is its death? The loss of all for which it lived, faded beauty, a broken form, hurled from a proud and peaceful height into the mire of the street, a dishonoured and pitiable wreck. Nay, what *is* the life of the leaf? The teacher tells the child: To nourish the stock that bore it; to prepare abundant supplies for the life and the labours of man; the fuel that warms, the fruit that feeds, the roof that shelters, the vehicles of commerce by land and sea that draw the nations into one, the sanctuaries vocal with a nobler praise than that which is warbled through the forest arches. It is to cleanse and vivify the vital air, and thus preserve in healthy vigour the blood of man and beast. It is to send the rain upon the pastures that feed the cattle on a thousand hills, and on the cornfields that nourish the great family of man. What, then, is its death? It is the fulfilment of the good end it lives for, a growing hard and brown in beneficent work, a ripening through constant usefulness into the many-coloured tints of splendid autumn, a putting-on of the God-given decorations of ennobled labour; it is a settling into an honoured grave all purpled like a king; it is a resigning of an outworn form to that Providence which treasures up each particle of faithful dust to enter into fresh forms of life and beauty in coming springs.

How plainly we see here—and this is the fact on which we must fix our thoughts to receive the spiritual lesson — that *different ideas of the purpose of the life lead to different ideas of what the death really is.* If we would transform our thought of death, we must transform our thought of life. It is the life that seems to exist only for itself, whose end is beset with those images of loss and degradation and melancholy pity which the poets have grouped about the fading leaf. On the other hand, it is the life whose bloom and strength are spent wholly in serving the good ends of the Creator, the life that gives itself for the world in serving and blessing its fellow-creatures, whose age is invested with dignity, whose death is mantled with glory, whose grave is watched over by the hope of entrance into useful life beyond.

What, then, is your life? This sober question of Holy Writ is the question which the autumnal season with its emblematic glory of the seemingly fading, but really ripening leaf, addresses to each of us. In our answer to this question is involved the secret of our future both here and hereafter. It is they who tell us that life is in ease and enjoyment, whose hopes are turned to gloom and dust, who are devoured with vain regrets and forebodings at the end, when life's voyage seems to reach no fair haven, but rather a rock-bound, unlighted, and storm-lashed coast. It is they who answer that life is in character, in faithful effort to discharge God's trusts, in seeking the good of others, the peace of conscience, and the Father's *Well done;* who come to the end as the soldier crowned with victory, who pillows his head on the joy of those who have fought the good fight, and closes his eye in hope of the triumphant to-morrow.

But there are lives that end when they have scarce begun. Fathers and mothers, bending over tiny graves, are tearfully asking why the leaf to fade so early should ever have opened in their home. Surely not that a cypress should ever be twined in all their garlands! Not that a bitterness otherwise unknown should ever be tasted in their cup! In that mere cradle-life there was a purpose, a mission, in recognising which the shortest life is seen to be well worth the living, and in its end a higher consolation than in saying, "The child is better off." Not to be loved for weeks, but to be loved for ever, came the babe. How many parents will bless God for ever for the babes that only came and went, as His angels, to bid them *lay hold on eternal life!* For how many benighted souls it has been a baby hand that has turned the key of the golden gate, and disclosed the light in the Father's open door, and drawn them after it into the deathless fellowship of the loving and the pure!

There are also other leaves that fall before 'tis nature's time to fade. The tree all summer long drops tribute prematurely on the soil. There are children just grown to be companions and helpers, who vanish from our side like leaves that fall in June. There are strong arms and loving hearts of wedded partners in life's burdens, that we suddenly miss from their places under the hot suns of toiling middle life. Many there are, who, having borne the midsummer heats, we expect will enjoy the tranquil dignity of a slowly ripening autumnal period, but all too early seem to lose their hold on earth, like the precocious leaf-falls of September. But how shall we regard this constant dropping of the earthly life? Is it no more than a gloomy succession of deserted rooms, disused garments, emptied seats, joys untasted, plans unfinished, good undone? Ask rather, what and Whom they lived for. Did they regard God's mission? Did they humbly eye the will of Him that sent them, and the good works which He " *before ordained that we should walk in them* "? Then, however few or many years, they did live long enough. Of one such it was anciently said: "He being made perfect in a short time fulfilled a long time." Deeds, not days, are God's measure of our life. And many, who do not live out half their days, yet see a good old age in deeds of usefulness. And whatever their special mission—whether, as a mere child, to make some fair example of filial obedience and devotion, or, as a patient mother, to rear and guide a family in the ways of

Christ, or by honest labour to find bread for a household and resources for charity, or to preach the Gospel, or to organise grand agencies of benevolence, or to rule a State—they had achieved God's purpose, they had lived long enough and well enough for Him, and therefore for themselves and for us, though their leaf faded in the bloom of its loveliness or the prime of its usefulness. For they had solved life's problem; they had learned how to live,

As ever in the great Taskmaster's eye.

And just as the Master is ever transferring His servants from work they have outgrown to tasks that will more fully exercise their powers in the present life, so, when God finds that His servant has learned how to live, how to employ his talent to the praise of Him that lent it, He oft translates him, even from work that seems to cry out for him, and from hearts that sadly miss him, to a sphere of service where ampler duties yield a revenue of nobler joys. Why, then, sigh for the past, when the leaf thus fades?—the work so well and quickly done, the reward so well and quickly come!

The text well brings a word of comfort also to aged Christians, whose leaf, though faded, has not fallen. Often do they miss their early vigour, and sigh that they seem to be useless, and think perhaps that the rushing world jostles them aside as in its way. Not so. Look at the leaf as it glows in October suns. God gave it that beauty as the crown of a well-spent life, which He permits to rest from its labours awhile before it sinks to earth. The ordinary uses of existence all fulfilled, its natural end well answered, God now bids it live a little longer, free from work, to serve a spiritual purpose. We love to contemplate it as a thing of beauty. It stirs our souls with thoughts that rise above the level of the work-life it has outlived. It teaches us those lessons of duty and of consolation which we to-day have been receiving. And so, says the Scripture, "*The hoary head is a crown of glory, if it be found in the way of righteousness.*" We love to read its "*living epistle*" of the faith that has overcome the world, of a serene "*peace with God through our Lord Jesus Christ,*" of the hope that "*maketh not ashamed,*" knows Whom it has believed, and looks forward to Him whom, not having seen, it loves. An aged and enfeebled Christian useless! Never! If, after more than forty centuries, it was written of Abel that, by his faith "*he, being dead, yet speaketh,*" how speaks to us the peaceful, hopeful waiting of the silvered heads of saints that sit with us in the sanctuary and salute us in the street; silent preachers they of "*the grace of God that bringeth salvation;*" lights are they in a world that is blessed by their quiet, holy shining!

Finally, since each of us must say to himself, I too do fade as a leaf, let us note with heed, whether the thoughts thus stirred within us are thoughts of hope and peace. If we hear it only as an unwelcome admonition of a melancholy limit, let us make certain that it is merely because of that instinctive dread of death, which God has appointed to be as a guardian angel to our life, and not from any lack of that Christlike aim, which life must recognise and realise, so that the due fading time may ripen the unfading hope.

But many there are, whose aim in life seems bent more on acquiring things to lose than things to keep; many whose last record is fuller of what they have left behind than of what they have carried hence of lasting gain. Many are the capacities to which this world gives exercise, but one only whose development carries with it the assurance of blissful exercise in a future world. It is the capacity for serving God in unselfish service of our fellows. This it is which visibly invests earth's fading time with life's autumnal splendours. This it is which invisibly forms under life's dropping leaf the bud which surely presages another spring. For us the one thing needful is to love this Christly and eternal life of service, for it is what we love that constitutes us what we become, and measures our future hope as solvent rather than insolvent souls.

Be it, then, our daily aspiration to be rich in good works, rich in the faith by which such works are wrought, rich toward God, rich in the things of the spirit rather than in the things of the flesh, rich in what we can carry hence as for ever ours, than in what we must leave behind to others. In a Divine present only can we find the sure pledge of a Divine future. Fade, then, when our leaf may, the end of earth will be to us not an unclothing, but a clothing upon, because "*mortality shall be swallowed up of life.*"

A Talk on Immortality.

WE were sitting in starlight by the window on a summer evening, talking of the immensities of Space, into which we were looking. Naturally this led into talk of the immensities of Duration, especially as affecting ourselves. Can it be true, said one of our group, that we, who are here in life now, shall be in life, say, a million trillion centuries from now, in continuity of individual consciousness with our present selves? It may be, was the answer. We do not know enough to deny it; neither do we know enough to assert it. If we appeal to the Scriptures, they do not assert it. They promise "eternal life"; but this, as the Nicene Creed shows, means only "the life of the world to come," without defining its duration. Eternal life denotes a kind of life rather than a length of life. It is a qualitative, not a quantitative term.

Upon this a conversation ensued upon immortality, the points of which were as follows:

Immortality properly denotes our indestructibility by the death of our physical organism. Of so much we may be assured. The same logic by which we accept the reality of the luminiferous ether, simply as a postulate of reason for the interpretation of the phenomena of light, requires us to accept the reality of immortality, as a postulate of reason for the interpretation of the moral phenomena of human life. A good man is an irrefragable argument for it. The materialist's conclusion is incredible—

> The forces that were Christ
> Have taken new forms and fled.

But is this life, so indestructible by the death of the body, a persistent life? Still more, is it endlessly persistent? The Scriptures affirm the resurrection, *both of the just and of the unjust.* Both alike rise up from the dying body into the life of the future. For the one it is a sound and well-conditioned life; for the other it is the reverse. The better conditioned, sounder, life should be, it would seem the more persistent also. Yet even for this, reason admits that what has had a beginning is, at least, liable to have an end. What, then, do we know that may shed a ray of probability upon the future life of the spirit as capacitated for an indefinite, perhaps an endless, continuance?

A mysterious and yet common fact of the present world is in its contrasts between a deficient and an exuberant vitality—the remarkable differences of individuals in their power to live. Some easily succumb to drains which others easily resist. In some families death comes early; in others late. The difference between the weak and the strong constitution is in their comparative vitality. Why it should be so faint in one, so vigorous in another, is not apparent. But we see that so it is. People are born so. Prenatal conditions have much to do with it. There are doubtless prenatal conditions to "the second birth of death" that produce similar effects. People are born into the next world, as into this, with differences of constitution or native vigour. Vitality may be be as variable in the spirit life as in the animal. As in the present state, so in the future, the duration of life may be conditioned in the power to live, to maintain an individualised existence in the sum of being.

Another fact of observation is that a feeble vitality in this world is enabled, by a well-directed vigilance and effort, to improve its chances, to recruit itself, and to subsist far longer than its apparent probabilities. On the other hand, we often see a strong vitality squandered by carelessness, and exhausted far short of its due period. Effort to live evidently enhances the power to live. Often is the spirit able, as Paul says, to "*quicken the mortal body,*" to make it live far beyond expectation. May we not deem it probable that the spirit's persistency in the future life is conditioned upon its effort to persist in the life-preserving way? What the Scriptures constantly affirm, all experience corroborates: "*Righteousness trusteth to life.*" Its way is the only life-preserving way. The struggle of conscience for righteousness is for a thing of eternal nature, in which there is no element of decay or dissolution.

Immortality, then, if we mean

by it not merely entrance into life after death, but also continuance therein, would seem to depend, in a degree at present indefinable, both upon the spirit's vitality, or power to live, and also upon its effort to live, by conserving or augmenting that power through perseverance in the life-preserving way. There are hints in the Scripture which look that way. "Incorruption"—in the A.V. "immortality"—is described as the prize of patience in well-doing. The eternal life is presented as something which we must "lay hold of."

The outlook which this course of thought leads to is not an assured prospect of existence strictly endless, in an individuality coeval with the life of God. It is more conceivable than this. It is a good hope of an indefinitely continued well-being achieved by due endeavour. It is enough for us that in the sound and healthy spiritual life no seeds of decay or death are apparent, and no limit is discoverable to its possibilities. Its goal in the ages of the ages is the Divine secret. But all that we can discover by the light of Scripture and Reason, or through experience and analogy, cautions us against thinking of life in the coming world as a gift any more unconditioned than life in the present. That life can be retained only in obedience to the laws of life, is doubtless true in all worlds. It is well to give the largest extension to our idea of immortality, provided we also give it its due moral significance for the inspiration of right living, by thinking of it as an achievement set before us to win, rather than as an endowment which we cannot lose.

Unspotted from the World.

THE sense which current Christian thought attaches to St. James's familiar phrase about keeping one's self "unspotted from the world" is by no means the same with the sense which it bears in his exhortation to an undefiled religious life. It is plainly a negative phrase, and warns us from forbidden ground. It seems to inculcate a certain avoidance and abstinence. If taken by itself, it is less suggestive of doing than of not doing, and of a standing aloof and on one's guard against the world rather than any mixing in encounter with the world. Hands off! keep your distance! seems to be its meaning—at least, if isolated from any connection that might modify the sense. This is the way it is generally taken, but, as will be seen, most mistakenly. And yet it is the most natural way to take it, as it stands in our Bibles. There it stands at the end of the chapter as a closing injunction, and in apparent contrast with words that enjoin philanthropic activity. *"Pure religion is to visit the fatherless and widows, and to keep one's self unspotted."* Here seem to be the two sides of life, benevolence outwardly, purity inwardly; charity with hands of bounty, and holiness scrupulously guarding the whiteness of its robes.

And yet there is hardly to be found a clearer case in which the Scriptures have been misunderstood, or misunderstood with greater detriment to Christian character. This exhortation to antagonise the selfishness, covetousness and inhumanity of the world—for such is its real import —has been construed as a caution to keep away from the contaminating touch of the world, especially in its soiling pleasures. This, indeed, is all-important; but it has escaped notice that this—which is not what St. James is speaking of—is involved in the other thing, which is really uppermost in his thought. The life of active philanthropy is far better safeguarded against desecrations by sinful self-indulgence than the life whose main endeavour is to keep clean from contact with things that defile.

It is a serious misfortune, therefore, that the injunction to keep unspotted from the world has been turned aside to a less consequential point than that it bears against in the Apostle's teaching. It is the favourite motto of those who proscribe the theatre, the ballroom, the game of cards, the dance. It is supposed to be realised by having nothing to do with certain amusements, or indulgences that are classified as worldly and inconsistent with a Christian profession; and yet nothing is plainer, as a matter of experience, than that the outside of the cup and platter may be kept clean, while the inside is full of an unclean and pharisaical spirit, intolerant, censorious, selfish. It is certain that St. James was thinking of no superficial matters, however important in their place they may be.

The break of his discourse at this critical point by the division of it into Chapter I. and Chapter II. is responsible for the unhappy misunderstanding. To see this, try to ignore the division, and read without a break. His subject just here is "pure religion," by which he means, as not only his original word, but also the old English use of the word "religion" shows, the active, not the contemplative, religious life—its outward liturgy, so to speak, rather than its inward spirit. What this is he defines both positively and negatively, as on one hand a ministration to the friendless and destitute—"the fatherless and widows"; and, on the other hand, as an avoidance of a surrounding defilement, from which one is to "keep oneself unspotted." But does he end here, and leave it to be conjectured what he means by this defiling spot? On the contrary, he goes right on to describe it at length. *"My brethren, hold not the faith of our Lord Jesus Christ, the Lord of glory, with respect of persons."* When you give a warm and obsequious greeting to the rich man who comes to your meeting, but to the poor man a cold and rude reception, you show the very plague-spot of the world's selfish materialism. You dishonour your Christian faith in the Lord of glory, when you esteem or despise men for what they have and wear.

Your denial of an equal brotherhood among the Lord's servants is a spot of pollution upon you from the anti-Christian world.

Manifestly now, in this view, the exhortation to keep unspotted requires a sort of endeavour much more positive and active than that of the mere negation and abstinence demanded by the view which refers it to the soiling pleasures of the world. If, in the Apostle's thought, the world's plague-spot is its unbrotherliness and inhumanity, this certainly can be avoided by no such rule as "touch not, taste not, handle not." Not to protest against it is to acquiesce in it. Non-interference is complicity. To permit it is to promote it. To be inactive in such a matter is to go with the priest and the Levite, who passed by the victim of the robbers. The only way to keep unspotted is to join hands with the good Samaritan.

The thought of St. James, thus

elicited and cleared of misunderstanding, has an eminent bearing on the subject which is sometimes brought up for discussion as the "secularisation of the Church." If, as we must hold in the true point of view, all things secular are sacred, because belonging to a world of which God is the sovereign, then it would seem that the concern of the Church is not with an unworldly or nonsecular class of interests, but rather to deal with all real or fancied human interests in an unworldy spirit. In other words, it is to carry into the stress and strain of the world's struggle the regenerating gospel of a Divine humanity that is given in the words "*Our Father*." The real and reprehensible secularisation of the Church is in its acquiescence with the selfish, secular policy of *laissez faire*, and allowing things that are unbrotherly and inhuman in the world's struggle to take their course, as demanded by the mere economist, or politician, or other remonstrants against the Church's turning aside from her work of "saving souls" to apply the law of Christ to legislators and statesmen and pleaders for vested rights.

We sometimes hear those who lament the "secularisation of the Church" desiderate what they call "the true note of the Gospel." This is just what we long to hear. But the note of the Gospel is most true when most closely related to the special need of the times for salvation from the sin of the times. Can any one who has thoughtfully looked upon the Church and the world in our time have any doubt that the sin which now dwarfs all others is *covetousness*? It is manifest in the family, where the talk and tone of "Christian" parents early teaches children to identify success in life with making money. It is manifest in the church, which rates its standing by the proportion of the well-to-do in its membership, rates its minister by his power to fill the pews with successful people, and, as in St. James's time, reserves the best seats for the best payers. It is manifest in society at large, where, not to speak of the frauds that taint business, the good cause that "has no money in it" has to bide its time in hope deferred. Not intemperance, not licentiousness, is a more deadly sin, more fatal to moral and spiritual life, than covetousness. But the note of severity with which the New Testament constantly names it, coupling it with the more disgusting vices, has died out of modern Christian speech; where it is seldom named except in a liturgical repetition of the Tenth Commandment, in phraseology that turns attention from the present to a bygone age.

But coveteousness, in the New Testament view, is not the wishing to take an ox or an ass from some neighbour. It is described as an undue wish for wealth in general, and a concentration of life upon the pursuit of it, instead of seeking the Kingdom of God. It is from this mammon spirit, which in its cheapening of goods is reckless of its cheapening of human lives, that the worst inhumanities of our times arise. The sin of the Church to-day is in its complicity with these, its blind tolerance both of the pernicious cause and the inhuman effect. And what more true or more Christlike note of the Gospel of the Son of Man could be sounded in the churches, hard by which a work of damnation is going on, than protests sharp enough, and prolonged enough, to shake smug respectability awake to consciousness that it is its brother's keeper, and in danger of sharing his damnation through neglect of its charge?

Finally, if we will read through St. James's illustration of what he means by keeping unspotted from the world, we shall see that the detested spot is the practical denial of human brotherhood, and that the avoidance of it must be in standing forth for the brotherliness which accords to every man an equal opportunity. Equality of opportunity in the house of God is the special thing the Apostle insists on; but the house of God, in its largest sense, is the world that God has built for all men's home. The equalisation of opportunity to lead a truly human life in the world is the great moral, and therefore the great religious, question of the present day. The *laissez-faire* policy of the old Manchester economists is now sufficiently discredited in the university to find no favour in the Church. Interference with the interferences that balk the normal aspirations and endeavours of men is now the accepted principle of social science. The Church cannot give it up to the sociologists. To make unrelenting war on whatever hinders the moral development of human life must be a cardinal principle of the Church that is true to her mission of promoting the brotherhood of men in Christ and in God. Whatever promotes this rings with the true note of the Gospel in which Christ is preached. To preach Christ comprehensively, rather than narrowly, is to preach up a Divine humanity, and to preach down whatever hinders it. It is of small use to hold up the Cross of Christ without rebuking the practices that contradict it.

To do this adequately for the present blindness and confusion of thought, to expose and brand the giant covetousness, the materialistic temper of the times, as it deserves, would be, as St. Peter says, a beginning of judgment at the house of God. It might empty some pulpits; it might cause a painful sifting both of consciences and of churches, whose now unconscious secularisation it would indict; it would be resented by many who would clamour for what they call "the old Gospel," which they do not regard as laying upon them any cross of active and self-denying concern for the bettering of miserable men. But it would be a true forward movement, the like of which has not yet been seen; for it would begin to give concrete reality to that apostolic thought of keeping unspotted from the world, which in the modern Church is in danger of a lingering death in a traditional and hollow phrase.

The Hidden Face.

Thou shalt see **My back**; but My face shall not be seen.—Exodus xxxiii. 23.

The natural is ever the matrix, the medium of the spiritual. Through men's faces we are wont to read their thoughts and hearts. Through the face feeling, intelligence, and will are revealed, and the spirit goes forth in expression. Such a fact at once clears up the enigmatic character of the dark saying in which the Word of God came to Moses. The thoughts and purposes of God cannot be discerned beforehand, as by one who reads another's face. They are discernible only afterward, when we contemplate the events in which these purposes passed on before us without recognition at the time.

It may at first seem that this is contradicted by the fact of prophecy so often verified. On the contrary, this fact fully bears us out. For what is it that prophecy foresees in its

> spiritual presentiments,
> And such refraction of events
> As often rises ere they rise?

Simply an event as a coming event, but not at all in its inner connections of cause and effect, how it is to come to pass, and what is to come of it, and its relations to other events in the world movement. In so foreseeing an event the Divine purpose therein is not seen; the face of God is veiled. So the overthrow of the Turkish tyranny has long been prophesied. Long as it is delayed, our assurance of it grows. But in the prophetic forecast certainty is limited to the mere event; the manner, the means, the time, the concomitants, the consequences, all the rational relations of it to other events in the unfolding of the historical order, and what it means for mankind in the purpose of God, will be inscrutable until God has passed by us in His unfolding of that order. So the coming of the Christ was foreseen in prophecy for centuries. And yet how different the real Christ from the anticipated, and how different the actual from the hoped-for consequences to Israel of His coming!

There is no more constantly-recurring fact of human experience than this inability to see the face and discern the thought of God, even in the nearest approach of the great turning-points of His providential control. When the Roman empire was on the verge of dissolution, when the birth-hour of Protestantism was at hand, when the Puritan exodus to New England was in progress, when the long preparing mine of the French Revolution was about to explode, when the downfall of slavery in the American Civil War was near, how thick lay the veil on the face of the Disposer of events! Even the Divinely-gifted Son of Man, who alone foresaw unerringly the sweeping away of the Temple, and Moses' seat therein, followed by His own enthronement as the spiritual lawgiver, declared that the hour not even the Son, but only the Father, foreknew.

Even now the signs are multiplying that we are nearing another turning-point in the movement of the world. The old militant order of things, both in nationalism and in industrialism, shows signs of breaking up and giving place to a pacific order, in which reason is to supplant force, and benign co-operation banish fierce competition. But the eternal cloud still covers the face of Providence. Only by the event shall we know the reality of His purposed transformation, and whether it is to be realised peacefully, or through such agony as has attended the epochal births of the past.

> For all the past of time reveals
> A bridal dawn of thunder peals,
> Whenever Thought hath wedded Fact.

Not only do we fail to read the Divine thought in the face of the imminent future, but also in that of the actual present. Hence, what blindness to precious opportunity, what blind fighting against God in opposing and persecuting His heralds, His bringers of better things! No sort of human inability is more general than that of discerning the inner significance of the time in which one lives. So, when the greatest spiritual force ever manifested on earth had entered the world in Jesus, how blind were all the wise to the fact that they were face to face with the power that was to subvert all opposing power! The history of the perverse Stuart kings is mainly a record of inability to read the face of their own times. Are the men of to-day more intelligent? The rarest penetration of our minds is into the pregnant, hidden significance of the events taking place in the social movement that goes on around us, so as to discern what God is bringing to birth through His inscrutable immanent control of what we call "natural causes."

The ancient saying is verified also in the history of science and its endeavours to discover God. It comes upon Him only from behind. It finds only footprints, which show it that the Creator has passed that way. It beholds His back, sees Him in the path He has taken, and the works He has wrought. It is only the eye of sense, the scientific eye, like the eye of Moses in the flesh, which is thus limited. The eye of the spirit discerns the Father's face. The pure in heart see God in holy intuitions possible to them alone,

> When all the nerve of sense is numb,
> Spirit to spirit, ghost to ghost.

Thus, Jesus saw the face of God, and by that vision was "*filled unto all the fulness of God.*"

The experience of Moses is common to us all. We realise it in personal as in social life. Lightly we enter on courses and ventures that are to determine our whole career. We discover long afterward that the moment of thoughtless choice was the moment of destiny. In the approach of trial and under the stress of trouble we cannot see God's face. His benign purpose is not discerned. Not till afterward, when the faith and patience, the resourcefulness and courage, the moral and mental strength developed in our struggle, light up the retrospect, do we see that God has passed by, and in passing, laid His hand upon us, that power might flow into us from His touch.

Finally, the dark saying, now interpreted, is an instructive word for each new year, whether that which begins alike for all on the first of January, or that which begins for each of us on his own birthday. *"Thou shalt see My back; but My face shall not be seen."* Reminding us of our mental and moral limitations, it enjoins us to keep the ways of life open to the Spirit of God in the heart and thought of a receptive mind, freed, if so it may be, from the blinding prepossessions which reject new truth because not understood, and new opportunities because underrated. Reminding us also that only by the Divine result will the Divine purpose that specially concerns us be revealed, it enjoins us to wait in patience and hope, whenever God's face is hidden by the hand He lays upon us, as on Moses, while passing by. So will every dubious hour of the present shine in its real divineness, when we look back upon it after it has receded far enough into the past.

The Lord's Supper.

"As often as ye eat this bread, and drink the cup, ye proclaim the Lord's death till He come."—1 COR. xi. 26.

IN affirming this fact with Paul one must not affirm, or understand Paul as affirming, that the Lord's Supper symbolises only the death of the Lord. The point now to be made is, that this limitation of the Lord's Supper to a representation of the Lord's death, and that only, is mistakenly made, and that thus the Lord's Supper is the point of defect and consequent weakness in ordinary Protestantism.

All Christians, however, agree that the Lord's Supper is in some sense a memorial, a commemoration of Him; it is, as Paul affirms, *the bread of the Lord,* and *the cup of the Lord*, to be worthily partaken of only after the due self-scrutiny which issues in *discerning the Lord's body*, but making the unworthy partaker to be *guilty of the body and blood of the Lord*,—words which solemnly distinguish the Lord's bread and cup from every other bread and cup of which we partake. Seizing upon this obviously commemorative character of the Supper, Zwingli interpreted it too superficially, in the narrow and merely historical way in which upon any anniversary we look back to the unreturning past. But in a larger view commemoration may recall the past into the living present, to reveal its permanent principle and law. Jesus evidently intended the Supper to be so used, "*unto*" (not merely, as we misread it, *in*) *remembrance* of Him. But the ordinary Protestant view dwells altogether upon the past, and misses the significance of the Supper for the present.

From this results an impoverishment of spiritual power and life, if not indifference to that fundamental law of Christian life which the Supper symbolically sets forth. We need not fear that its historical reference to Christ's passion will be either forgotten or inadequately commemorated. The great thing which has been overlooked is its symbolical commemoration of Christ's life as the life to be lived by all who partake of it as in fellowship with Him.

Recall, then, the circumstances of the original institution. At the end of a life whose sympathies and services had been daily distributed in unselfish ministries to all, our Master took bread, and blessed and broke it, and distributed it to the table company, saying, " Take, eat; this is My body given for you." Could any rite more fitly symbolise, not His death only, but also His self-distributing, self-sacrificing life, of which His death was the final and befitting act? "*Do this,*" said He, "*unto remembrance of Me.*" The truth constantly forgotten, constantly to be recalled, is that the fittest commemoration is imitation. A life that had been perfected through a daily dying to all that stood in the way to the attainment of its end wishes to be commemorated in lives that obey its fundamental law of self-devotion to the Kingdom of God and His righteousness. So at the end of a ministry to human needs in which death in manifold forms of self-renunciation had been continually tasted by the sacrificial spirit, and on the night when the final form of death is reached, as the threshold of the perfected life of the spirit, our Master chooses for His sacramental emblem the bread. "It is My body"; it represents Me. How fitly chosen! The grain has passed through mill and fire to become our food. It sets forth the law of Jesus' life as the law of His followers' life. "Do this," He would say, "to remind yourselves to live as I have lived," the life that is purified from selfishness in the self-devoting distribution of its sympathies and powers to others' needs, the life that is perfected through self-sacrifice to the uttermost.

"Likewise also the cup." Here in another medium the same truth is mirrored. The symbolic significance of the cup does not essentially differ from that of the bread. The object-lesson is reiterated for emphasis. The two witnesses solemnise it indisputably. "This *bread is My body, this cup is My blood.*" The one broken for all, the other poured forth for all, each distributed to all, He declares representative of Himself; thus He symbolises His whole self—flesh and spirit—His entire life, freely devoted for the world. "*For the remission of sins,*" He added. The Epistle to the Hebrews repeats it: "*to put away sin by the sacrifice of Himself*"—words which denote not the mere pardon, but the abolition of sin. It is only through the sacrificial, self-devoting spirit that the "remission"—the putting away—of sin is accomplished by Jesus, and by whoever seeks with Jesus to loose men from the power of sin.

Such is the significance of the Supper as symbolic of the priesthood which the Master calls the disciple to fulfil in daily life. It is the solitary institution of the Founder of Christianity. Everything else called Christian has had a development. This is His unchanged and primitive witness. It owes all its sacramental significance to the facts of His life and death.

If we speak only of His death,

we must reckon this as the crowning act of His life. If we speak only of His life, we must regard this as continually what Paul calls a dying unto sin, and because of sin, in all the varied forms of selfishness. In its symbolism of these is its value for the quickening of the daily life, whose power for good is in the inspirations of its fellowship of sympathy with Him. To eat of His bread and drink of His cup is to signify our loyal and loving acceptance of the priestly life He lived, the all-serving, self-distributing life, the life which daily dies with Him to every form of mere self-seeking, in the daily laying down of itself for others—as the life for us to live, the life whose perfectness and divine blessedness are not in receiving but in giving.

The key to this view of the Supper is in Christ's words to James and John not long before: "The Son of Man came not to be ministered unto, but to minister, and to give His life a ransom for many." The ransom—the means of redemption, were not furnished only by His final laying down of life, but also by its daily laying down in the sacrificial ministrations of the self-devoting life. The older Protestant theologians seem to have recognised this in their teaching that Christ became our Saviour in virtue of His "active obedience" to law, as well as of His "passive obedience" to death. This active obedience, of course, was in that sacrificial bearing of each others' burdens, in which Paul calls upon us also to fulfil "the law of Christ," that is, the law which He obeyed. Nor can it be by Jesus solely, apart from His spirit in His co-operating disciples, that men are delivered from their sins. Our sacrifices, also, in addition to our Master's, are indispensable for this. He was paying this ransom all His days, as well as on His last day. This priestly work He left for us to follow up and finish.

The Lord's Supper is His appointed memorial to keep this fact ever before us. This it is which the Protestant churches overlook, with the result of weakness from their neglect of it. The idea of a present and perpetual sacrifice has ever been connected with it in the Christian conscience, however inadequately or superstitiously the idea may have been expressed. Witness the oblation of the Mass among Romanists, the table-offering for the poor among Protestants.

In the ministrations of self-devoting and Christly love to redeem men from their sins is the universal priesthood of the perpetually sacrificing Church. Of His own share in it, as our Great High Priest, Jesus said, "*It is finished.*" Of the share He left in it to His followers and helpers to the Kingdom of God, Paul said, speaking of himself, "*I fill up on my part that which is lacking of the afflictions of Christ.*"

The mystical language of the Calvinistic statement in the Westminster Confession, that in the Supper believers are "made partakers in Christ's body and blood" —that is, in Christ's own self and spirit, must be understood as affirming the disciples' fellowship with their Master in this priestly offering of self for others unto God. Here is the point of defect and weakness in the current Protestant conception of this sacrament. The regulative New Testament idea of the Christian life as a priesthood, a priestly life like that of Christ, is not perpetuated in the use of the Lord's Supper which He intended. The Lord's Supper, rightly treated as symbolic of the life which Jesus lived and calls us to live, is the witness to this forgotten truth of the universal priesthood. Until this comes to be better understood and realised, the pitiful pretensions of an ecclesiastical caste will continue, as now, to scandalise some and to delude others.

The great schism which has long afflicted the Church is between Priestism on the one hand, and Protestantism on the other. In its conflict with the heresy of Priestism, Protestantism is weakened by failure to do justice to the truth which Priestism recognises but perverts. This truth is the essentially priestly character and function to which every Christian is called. Not to Peter only, or a class of clergy only, as his exclusive successors, are given *"the keys of the kingdom of heaven,"* and the power to *"bind and loose."* The priestly function of freeing men from their sins is the function of Peter's faith that Jesus is the Son of God. To all who have obtained "*like precious faith*" with Peter does it belong. And so it is Peter himself who writes to his fellow-believers, "*Ye are a royal priesthood.*"

But Priestism perverts this fundamental truth by its arrogation of the priestly character and function to a single class of Christians—its clergy. Against this perversion the stronghold of the truth for which Protestantism contends is the Biblical idea of the Lord's Supper, as the sacramental memorial, in vivid symbols, of the priestly calling of every member of the Body of Christ to share with its Head in the sacrifices by which men are loosed from sin. But of this our current Protestantism makes little account. Consequently it still is weak at the very point where it is most strongly antagonized by Priestism.

We must, therefore, constantly reiterate and emphasize the truth that in the sacrament of the Lord's Supper the spiritually enlightened recipient devotes himself to that priestly life of unselfish ministration to others' good, wherein the disciple must follow the Master in the offering of those sacrifices which are effectual to set men free from their sins. Had this holy sacrament thus been thought of — had it not been thought of rather as exclusively pointing to a great sacrifice in the past, which requires no sacrifices in the present to give it efficacy for real redemptive power, what scandals of unreason and unrighteousness had never disgraced the Christian name!

However much, therefore, we deprecate Luther's polemic and uncharitable spirit in his quarrel with Zwingli about the Supper, we deem that it was a true, though a blind, instinct which prompted him to protest so pugnaciously, that this sacrament was more than the mere historical commemoration that Zwingli made it, as the Protestant churches seem now, for the most part, to agree with Zwingli in making it.

Affirming still, with Paul, that it is to "show the Lord's death," we must not restrict ourselves to that affirmation. We must not forget that He was laying down his life all His days in His expenditure of Himself for others, as really as He laid it down finally on His last day, always bearing in the spirit the cross which He bore once in the body. We have, therefore, to affirm also with Paul what is too often forgotten—the true disciple's partnership in his Master's death, described by such phrases as "We were baptised into His death," "We died with Christ." If the Supper symbolises the one, it symbolises the other also; it is a sacred reminder of the Christian's priestly calling to a daily laying down of life, in the sacrifice of all lower ends to the supreme end of realising the kingdom of heaven on the earth. The distribution of the broken bread and the outpoured wine shows forth in figure our Master's priestly example, as His demand upon us to be what He was and to do what He did, a demand for the reproduction of His life in our lives, a demand to be cherished "*unto*" that true remembrance of Him, which is commemoration by imitation, in the free impartation to the world of all that in us is— body and soul, flesh and spirit— that the Kingdom of God may come through a perpetual giving of the life of Christ in the lives of His disciples.

This is the reality of the Perpetual Sacrifice, which Romanists and Romanisers dimly conscious of it have misrepresented in the Mass. Only in our responsiveness to our Master's requirement of this does the

Supper become in fact, what it is in phrase, "the Communion"—in the identification of feeling with feeling, will with will, life with life, between the Master and the disciples. So viewed indeed, it becomes, as it is called, "the Holy Communion."

Thus viewed, the Lord's Supper is more than a mere commemoration of a historic death; it it equally a setting forth of a past and present life—as a life that involves a daily dying to all selfishness. Had it been so viewed, doubtless it would never have been discarded, as it has been, in some Protestant churches of the ultra-liberal sort, who have taken a narrow view of it as no more than a symbol of a special dogma concerning the Atonement which they repudiate. Nor would it in other churches be so often celebrated in a formal and almost perfunctory way, instead of being made, as the sacerdotal churches with a true though blind instinct make it, the central shrine, the crowning act of worship. The Lord's Supper is thus, in the highest sense, essentially a sacrament of life—the true priestly life of sacrifice, which is entered into and realised in faith's sympathetic fellowship with Christ—the life which is for to-day and forever, the life eternal,

Here, then, the Lord's Supper in its present import becomes prophetic, and points forward. Its significance is by no means exhausted when viewed in its historical connection and present bearing, vitally important as these are. But how poorly is its prospective pointing generally regarded! We have lost a most precious part of its meaning when we forget the salient fact that it was instituted on the verge of that great Shadow, where chill doubts arise lest the life that is seen no more should exist no more. Recall again the memorable circumstances. Instituted as it was, at the end of an intimate earthly fellowship, it originally embodied the idea of a fellowship transcending earth and surviving the grave. When the Master had saddened the table company by intimations of His impending decease, He added that His fellowship with them was not to be terminated, but rather translated. *"I go to prepare a place for you, that where I am there ye may be also." "Ye shall eat and drink at My table in My kingdom."* Thus He made the bread and the cup, which were the last of earth, to be a foretaste of heaven, and the sacramental symbols of an immortal hope, that the Christly life perfected through sacrifice shall pass through the Shadow into perpetual light.

Evidently it was to Him not an end merely, but equally a threshold, a line where the two worlds meet, a transition point between the communion which is limited to time and place, and the communion of the Spirit, in which one roof is felt as overspreading all the "mansions" of the Father's House. Viewing it thus with Him, the holy Supper, in this most obvious aspect of the facts of its institution, is manifestly a sacramental pledge of immortality. As such, it was precious in the primitive age, when the new truth of the Resurrection was newly astir. Likewise precious it deserves to be, so long as we behold our beloved ones ever vanishing from us into the depths of the inscrutable Shadow.

While, therefore, we cherish the pathos of its historic reference to our Master's death, and equally insist on its quickening power for the present, in its emblematic expression of His all-serving, self-devoting, priestly life, as the life to which His disciple is pledged in imitation of Him, we cannot without loss ignore what it gives us beyond this, in its inspiring prophecy of the indestructible life of the Christly spirit. If we but duly regard this, then, as often as we eat of the bread, and drink of the cup, we shall give thanks not only for the past, but for the future also. We shall feel our communion not only with our fellow-servants on earth, but also with the "ministering spirits" beyond the veil, in the "great cloud of witnesses" above us, as well as with the glorified Master and Head of all. Most aptly is this upward pointing of the Supper followed in the thanksgiving in the Communion Service in the Book of Common Prayer: "We bless Thy Name for all Thy servants departed this life in Thy faith and fear; beseeching Thee to give us grace so to follow their good examples, that with them we may be partakers of Thy heavenly kingdom." Here breathes the thought which Jesus inlaid in His institution of the Sacrament, that thought of deathless fellowship which burns in Wesley's tender lines:

One family we dwell in Him,
  One church, above, beneath,
Though now divided by the stream,
  The narrow stream, of death.
Even now by faith we join our hands
  With those that went before,
And greet the ransomed blessed bands
  Upon the eternal shore.

The subject has now been presented for reflection in its Biblical wholeness and proportion. That this is maintained in the ordinary conceptions of it few will contend. That loss of spiritual power, defect of spiritual life, and infidelity to the Christian ideal must result from either a partial or distorted apprehension of this unique and sole institution of the Master, is most certain. The proof of it is on the pages of church history, where this sacrament of life and immortality seems ever to be the provocative of discords, and the starting-point of anti-Christian hatreds.

Among the prerequisites to that reunion of the divided churches upon which so many hearts are set, none is of higher consequence than a revised and truly Biblical apprehension of the Lord's Supper in its threefold lesson of the past, the present, and the future — a sacramental representation of the Christian life, both as rooted in Christ, and lived with Him both here and hereafter. It is widely felt among Protestants that the great hindrance to reunion is in the arrogantly exclusive doctrine of Priestism. What needs to be no less widely felt is the certainty that Priestism will continue to work for schism, so long as the truth, on the perversion of which it lives — the priestly character and function of the whole Body of Christ, and of every member thereof, fails to receive among Protestants the recognition and emphasis given to it in the sacrament of the Lord's Supper.

Perhaps it is not too much to say that if Christian people had been as intent on truth to practise as on truth to discuss, the sacrament would never have been outranked by the creed, as it is among most Protestants. Perhaps it is not too much to hope that men grown weary of the subtleties of the creed may rediscover in the sacrament the original and effective exponent of the truths most vital for the power and the hope of the Christian life, in securing it from the blight of Pharisaism on one hand, and of Agnosticism on the other.

Meanwhile, there still is a mission for the Sacerdotalist, insisting that men are saved by sacraments, which must be administered by those who have an exclusive prerogative to stand as priests between men and God. By this perversion of truth a needful service is done in calling the Protestant's attention to the truth which is overlooked. The sacerdotalist is blindly right in affirming that there is much more in the Lord's Supper than the Protestant usually finds. His unfounded pretensions can be overcome only by that complete presentation of the truth, without defect and without excess, for which the anti-sacerdotal churches still wait. Because of the weakness of the current Protestantism at this point, its conflict with Sacerdotalism, whether Romanist or Anglican, is still at issue. And it is not too much to say, that a reinforcement of Protestant teaching at this weak but vital point is indispensable, if its lingering conflict is ever to have a successful issue.

In view also of the struggle of the spirit of Christianity with the antichristian influences that still afflict society and infest the churches, it may be affirmed with confidence that no one line of advance in Christian truth promises more for a revival of spiritual power, and the rejuvenescence of the primitive vigour and purity of the unselfish Christian life, than for the reformed churches to revise and round out in Biblical fulness their doctrine of the Lord's Supper.

Gymnastics and Ascetics.

A VITAL difference between gymnastics and ascetics has been obscured in our Bibles, with loss to Christian thought and power. Gymnastics is exercise for development. Ascetics is exercise for repression. This difference appears in comparing Paul's exhortation to Timothy, "*Exercise thyself unto godliness,*" and his declaration before Felix, "*I exercise myself to have a conscience void of offence.*" In the former Paul's Greek work (*gumnaze*) denotes gymnastic exercise; in the latter (*asko*), ascetic.

That Christian endeavour has been exercised in repression rather than in development is significantly intimated by the fact that *ascetic* is naturalised in our religious vocabulary, while *gymnastic* has no place therein. Christian morality still runs largely on the negative line of Judaic legalism, "*Thou shalt not,*" and but moderately on the positive line of the Beatitudes. A large part of Christendom still emphasizes the annual religious revival called "Lent" by exercising itself in special abstinence, rather than by special insistence, such as the fifty-eighth chapter of Isaiah requires for the "*acceptable fast,*" on works of justice and mercy.

Here is the cause of the moral weakness and degeneration that afflict the churches to-day. Much of their goodness is of the ascetic rather than of the gymnastic kind. Its type is in the negative righteousness of the Scribes and Pharisees, rather than in the positive righteousness of Christ.

The recovery of the long-obscured truth of the real humanity of Christ has already in part restored to Christian consciousness its long-neglected companion-truth, the imitableness of the moral excellence of Christ. This is the sole line of Christian power to overcome the world by redeeming the world. Already, as Dr. Gordon* has said, "the conduct and spirit of Christian nations are under the stimulus and rebukes of the moral standard of Christ." But the world, whose conscience thus does homage to Christian theory, lies in wickedness for lack of the Christian practice that should enforce it. Nor can the Church any longer give a valid reason for her existence in any distinction from the world, except as a society for the practical illustration of Christ's theory of life.

To effect this she must do far more than practise the negative precepts which He took over from Moses. Gymnastic, not

* In his book, *The Christ of To-day.*

ascetic morality is required of her. She must go forward in the school of Christ, master the advanced lessons, pursue the higher courses, go through the university training, exercise herself in the purer righteousness, the finer charity, the more heroic self-sacrifice, the diviner consciousness of her Master. This Divine morality can be successfully cultivated only as it is identified with religion. It is, indeed, one with "*pure religion and undefiled before our God and Father.*"

This is what Lent is for, if it is for anything worth attaining. Whatever subsidiary value there may be in ascetic exercises of abstinence to promote a devout remembrance of the self-denial of Christ, may be freely recognised and sought. But the essential exercise of the genuinely Christian spirit is not in these, however these may aid it. It is rather in steadfast gymnastic endeavour to reproduce Christ's life of active goodness and Christ's Divine service at the various altars of human need, by the religiously moral effort to obey His law, that *"the disciple must be as his Master, and the servant as his Lord."*

Jesus' Coming Again.

THE season which calls to mind the coming of Jesus into the world calls to mind that coming again of which He spoke, which for nineteen centuries has been a subject both of anticipation and perplexity. As to this, it is a fair question whether those who make it a reproach to Jesus, as indicating lack of mental sanity, do not too hastily take up with the opinions of His contemporaries as to what He meant. Great minds are regularly misunderstood by the inferior minds around them, and Jesus was certainly no exception to the rule.

But the fact that His disciples confidently anticipated His coming again in their lifetime to judge a world enslaved to its sins requires us to ask, Is it antecedently more probable that Jesus Himself so believed, and taught them so, or had He no such idea, and did they get it elsewhere? In view of Jesus' conspicuous reasonableness in other points, the latter alternative certainly puts the least strain on our powers of belief.

With this presumption in mind, we observe a marked difference between the Synoptics and the Fourth Gospel on the subject of Jesus' coming again. The latter represents it as of an inward and spiritual sort; the former set it forth as apocalyptic and spectacular. Again, we have to ask as to the antecedent probability of each of these divergent representations. In view of the fact that the Jewish mind had long been imbued with the ideas formed by Apocalyptic writings concerning the advent of a national Messiah, the disciples could have got the idea of a spiritual coming only from Jesus: it must have been His own.

But, if this is so, what could Jesus have said which accounts for the Apocalyptic advent prophecies attributed to Him? It was, doubtless, the prediction He is admitted to have made of the fall of the holy city and its temple during the lifetime of some who heard Him. This, certainly, was one of the long series of judgment days which history records. Such a " day of the Lord " the Hebrew prophets had invested with imagery hyperbolical to us, but common to Orientals, symbolising the quenching of the great lights of the Church and State as the extinction of the luminaries of the firmament. To borrow such imagery to describe the impending eclipse of Judaism would be simply natural for a mind saturated with the ancient Scriptures, as the mind of Jesus was.

If, now, one considers that the eclipse of Judaism was the revelation of Christianity as distinct from it, and that Jesus looked forward to the rising of the new faith as the old faith declined, it is easy to account, on the foregoing grounds, for a transformation in the disciples' minds of what Jesus said into what they thought. In their thought, His idea of a spiritual coming and enthronement as a Divine lawgiver, in Moses' stead, was transformed into the Apocalyptic Idea of His visible return to the world as its judge. At any rate, the alternative lies between the easier view that the disciples, with their Jewish prepossessions, translated Jesus' spiritual thought, here as elsewhere, into mechanical forms, and the far more difficult belief that Jesus here descended to the level of the current ideas concerning the advent of the Messiah.

It seems most reasonable to think that, here as elsewhere, Jesus may be better understood by us than by His contemporaries. The proof needs to be overwhelming which would convict Him of such a lack of sanity as would be involved in His believing that, in the course of a few years, He would come again, begirt with clouds and escorted by angels, to judge mankind. But some of His characteristic sayings, as the parables of the leaven and of the secretly growing seed, show an utterly opposite thought of His great cause. Says Dr. E. Caird, in his "Evolution of Religion," "It is not too much to say that, in some of His words, the idea that true progress is possible only by development is more clearly expressed than it ever was by any one down to the present century, when it has become the key-note of all speculation."

The coming again that Jesus thought of is evolutionary, not catastrophic; in spirit, not in form; precisely as He Himself described Elijah as having come again to earth in the dauntless and austere spirit of John the Baptist. And yet the Church, in its hymns, its liturgies, and its creeds, is still, with the men of Galilee, looking up into heaven for a miraculous descent of the Christ, instead of that spiritual ascent within the heart and conscience which depends on our furtherance to hasten its rise. This it is which the Christmas season, amid all its retrospective suggestions, calls us mainly to think on, the better to promote the real and Divine advent. It is the incoming into power among men of Jesus' Divine humanity, in that true humanising which is also the Divinising of religion, habits, institutions, laws, our thoughts of God, our thoughts and treatment of one another. To see what there is of this already in the world is to get hope that there shall be more of it, and encouragement for the effort which makes hope effectual.

www.ingramcontent.com/pod-product-compliance
Lightning Source LLC
Chambersburg PA
CBHW030337170426
43202CB00010B/1157